12-17

HEALTH SCIENCES

Exploring Career Pathways

Diane Lindsey Reeves

Created and produced by
Bright Futures Press, Cary, North Carolina
www.brightfuturespress.com

Published by
Cherry Lake Publishing, Ann Arbor, Michigan
www.cherrylakepublishing.com

Photo Credits: Cover, BeautyLine; page 7, Tyler Olson, VGstockphoto, Kzenon, Stock-Asso, Minierva Studio, stefanolunardi, Ocskay Mark, Alexander Raths; page 8, Kzenon; page 10, Tyler Olson; page 12, Stock-Asso, page 14, Ocskay Mark; page 16, Minerva Studio; page 18, Alexander Raths; page 20, stefanolunardi; page 22, VGstockstudio; page 24, denira.

Library of Congress Cataloging-in-Publication Data

Names: Reeves, Diane Lindsey, 1959- author.
Title: Health sciences / Diane Lindsey Reeves.
Description: Ann Arbor, Michigan : Cherry Lake Publishing, [2017] I Series:
   World of work I Audience: Grades 4 to 6. I Includes bibliographical
   references and index.
Identifiers: LCCN 2016042180I ISBN 9781634726245 (hardcover) I ISBN
   9781634726443 (pbk.) I ISBN 9781634726344 (pdf) I ISBN 9781634726542
   (ebook)
Subjects: LCSH: Medical sciences--Vocational guidance--Juvenile literature. I
   Medical personnel--Juvenile literature.
Classification: LCC R690 .R4415 2017 I DDC 610.69--dc23
LC record available at https://lccn.loc.gov/2016042180

Printed in the United States of America.

TABLE OF CONTENTS

HELLO WORLD OF WORK

This is you.

Right now, your job is to go to school and learn all you can.

This is the world of work.

It's where people earn a living, find purpose in their lives, and make the world a better place.

Sooner or later, you'll have to find your way from **HERE** to **THERE**.

To get started, take all the jobs in the incredibly enormous world of work and organize them into an imaginary pile. It's a big pile, isn't it? It would be pretty tricky to find the perfect job for you among so many options.

No worries!

Some very smart career experts have made it easier to figure out. They sorted jobs and industries into groups by the types of skills and products they share. These groups are called career clusters. They provide pathways that will make it easier for you to find career options that match your interests.

Architecture & Construction

Arts & Communications

Business & Administration

Education & Training

Finance

Food & Natural Resources

Government

Health Sciences

Hospitality & Tourism

Human Services

Information Technology

Law & Public Safety

Manufacturing

Marketing

Science, Technology, Engineering & Mathematics (STEM)

Transportation

Good thing you are still a kid.

You have lots of time to explore ideas and imagine yourself doing all kinds of amazing things. The **World of Work** (WoW for short) series of books will help you get started.

TAKE A HIKE!

There are 16 career pathways waiting for you to explore. The only question is: Which one should you explore first?

Is **Health Sciences** a good path for you to start exploring career ideas? There are many important opportunities to be found along this pathway. Professionals in this field **diagnose** and treat diseases. They take care of us when we are sick and operate on us when our bodies break down. They keep our teeth healthy. They discover lifesaving new medicines. And so much more.

See if any of the following questions grab your interest.

WOULD YOU ENJOY nursing a sick pet back to health, dissecting animals in a science lab, or helping the school coach run a sports clinic?

CAN YOU IMAGINE someday working at a dental office, hospital, or veterinary clinic?

ARE YOU CURIOUS ABOUT what art therapists, doctors, dentists, pharmacists, and veterinarians do?

If so, it's time to take a hike! Keep reading to see what kinds of opportunities you can discover along the Health Sciences pathway.

But wait!

What if you don't think you'll like this pathway?

You have two choices.

You could keep reading, to find out more than you already know. You might be surprised to learn how many amazing careers you'll find along this path.

OR

Turn to page 27 to get ideas about other WoW pathways.

EMERGENCY MEDICAL TECHNICIAN

VETERINARIAN

NUTRITIONIST

WoW Up Close

Deliver babies. Discover cures for **cancer** and other life-threatening diseases. Set broken bones and repair broken hearts. These are just some of the important things people who work along the Heath Science pathway do.

ATHLETIC TRAINER

SURGEON

PHYSICIAN'S ASSISTANT

PSYCHOLOGIST

ORTHODONTIST

ATHLETIC TRAINER

When sports are played, people get hurt. It is part of the game. Sports involve pushing the human body to its limit. Bones get broken. Muscles get strained, sprained, and torn. When people run, jump, tackle, and perform other high-energy feats, injuries are bound to happen.

Athletic trainers keep players in tip-top shape in three ways. They treat injuries that occur during practice or games. They help players recover from injuries to get them back in the game. And they work really hard to prevent injuries from happening in the first place.

You may have noticed athletic trainers at work on the sidelines during a game. They are always prepared to do first aid and provide emergency care. Before games start, they stay busy taping knees, ankles, and wrists. During games, they make sure players get plenty of fluids. After games, they ice down and massage sore muscles. Every player has a prescribed plan based on their specific needs.

Athletic trainers go to college and must earn at least a degree in athletic training or sports medicine. They also must pass a special exam and be licensed by the National Athletic Trainers' Association. Then they can start working with athletes.

Check It Out!

See athletic trainers in action at

- http://bit.ly/AthTrainer
- http://bit.ly/SportsTrainer

Start Now!

- Be on the lookout for athletic trainers at work when you watch professional sports games on TV.

- Take a first aid class. Check for classes offered through your local Red Cross at http://www.redcross.org.

- Go to the Web site of your favorite professional sports team or league for the latest news on injured players.

EMERGENCY MEDICAL TECHNICIAN

If you are ever in an accident or face a medical crisis, you will want an **emergency medical technician (EMT)** to come to your rescue. These trained professionals rush to accidents, disasters, and other emergencies to provide immediate, on-the-scene care.

EMTs might arrive in an ambulance or a specially equipped helicopter. Either way, the goal is to provide quick and capable care until the patient can be transported to a medical center. Saving lives is often part of a day's work for EMTs.

EMT training starts with a high school diploma and cardiopulmonary resuscitation (CPR) training. From there, EMTs must successfully complete one to two years of EMT training at a community college or technical. These programs train EMTs how to determine a patient's condition and calmly handle all kinds of emergencies. Every day on the job brings new challenges that range from car accidents to heart attacks.

Paramedics also provide emergency care. The difference between an EMT and a paramedic is that paramedics have completed more advanced training. Future EMTs and paramedics can get a head start on training by taking anatomy and physiology courses in high school.

Check It Out!

Follow EMTS and paramedics around online at

▸ http://bit.ly/ParaEMT

▸ http://bit.ly/ParaEMT2

Start Now!

✓ Take a CPR class at your local community center or through the American Heart Association (http://cpr.heart.org).

✓ Visit your local fire department and ask to talk to someone with EMT training.

✓ Go online to find basic first aid tips for dealing with common injuries like burns, bee stings, black eyes, and choking.

NUTRITIONIST

You are what you eat. Eat healthy and you increase your chances of staying healthy. Eat too much junk food and your health suffers. You gain too much weight and **obesity** happens. Your chances of getting a disease called **diabetes**, having a heart attack, and even getting certain types of cancer increase.

Nutritionists are health professionals who help people make better choices about food. They might work with people who want to lose or gain weight. They create special diets needed by people who have certain health conditions like diabetes or high blood pressure.

Nutritionists work in hospitals, cafeterias, nursing homes, weight loss clinics, and schools. Some also work for professional sports teams where good nutrition helps keep athletes in tip-top shape.

The challenge for all nutritionists is getting people to change bad habits and make better choices. This can involve setting up meal plans, teaching patients about health risks, and introducing them to new types of foods. Sometimes people are surprised to discover how much they enjoy healthy foods once they try them. The best part of being a nutritionist is helping people feel better, look better, and live longer.

It's never too soon to start preparing for a career as a nutritionist. You can take health and family and consumer studies classes at school. You can also learn to prepare healthy meals at home.

Check It Out!

Find all kinds of nutrition resources for kids at

▶ http://www.choosemyplate.gov

▶ http://www.letsmove.gov

Start Now!

- ✔ Create a collage on a paper plate to show how to eat healthy.

- ✔ Make a list of 10 healthy snacks.

- ✔ Visit the produce department of your local grocery store and see how many new kinds of fruits and vegetables you discover.

ORTHODONTIST

An **orthodontist** is a dentist who specializes in straightening crooked teeth. Crooked teeth or jaws can cause problems. It might become painful for a person to chew or swallow. Jaws that are out of line can cause headaches and muscle pain. Problems with teeth and jaws can make it difficult for people to sleep or speak properly.

Of course, one of the biggest reasons why people go to see orthodontists is because their teeth look unattractive. By straightening teeth, orthodontists give people beautiful smiles.

After examining patients, orthodontists come up with treatment plans. They use braces, retainers, headgear, and other techniques to fix the problems they discover. It can take months or even years to achieve the desired results. Patients must return to the orthodontists for regular adjustments.

If you want to become an orthodontist, there is good news and bad news. The "bad" news is that it takes more than 10 years of training to become an orthodontist. That includes four years of college, four years of dental school, and two or three years of special orthodontic training. The good news is that a good orthodontist earns a much higher than average salary. This can make that big investment in education pay off.

Check It Out!

Find out how braces work at

▶ http://bit.ly/BracesWork

▶ http://bit.ly/OrthoDay

Start Now!

✔ Humans have 32 permanent teeth. They include **incisors**, **canines**, **bicuspids**, and **molars**. Use markers or modeling clay to make a model of a mouth and use different colors to show each type of tooth.

PHYSICIAN'S ASSISTANT

Physician's assistants, or PAs, examine, diagnose, and treat patients. They put casts on broken limbs, stitch up wounds, and order medical tests. They even prescribe medicines. PAs work in doctor's offices, clinics, and hospitals.

In fact, PAs do many things that doctors do. So what's the difference between a PA and a doctor?

The biggest difference is training. It can take up to 15 years to prepare to practice certain types of medicine. Training for all doctors includes four years of college, four years of medical school, and a three- to five-year residency. Some specialists also complete a one- or two-year **fellowship** before becoming licensed. Training to become a doctor requires a huge commitment of time and education costs.

On the other hand, PAs get a college degree and then must go to work in health care for at least three years. Then they go back to college for three years of training in special physician's assistant programs.

The shorter training time is why PAs must perform their duties under the supervision of a licensed medical doctor. It is also why many consider the job to be one of the most promising careers in America. PAs are in high demand. They fill a huge need for health care professionals to care for a growing and aging population.

Check It Out!

Ever wonder what a physician's assistant does? Find out at

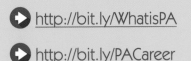

http://bit.ly/WhatisPA

http://bit.ly/PACareer

Start Now!

- ✔ Practice being a PA by finding out all you can about common childhood illnesses like colds, strep throat, and the flu. What are the symptoms? What can you do to feel better when you get illnesses like these? Use the Internet and library resources to find out more, and jot down details for each illness on index cards.

PSYCHOLOGIST

Psychology is the study of the mind, emotions, and human behavior. A **psychologist** is a medical professional who deals with how people think, feel, and act. They help people better understand why they do the things they do.

There are many reasons why someone might see a psychologist. A person might be feeling down or stressed out. Maybe something really bad has happened, and the person needs help coping. Psychologists also help people who are struggling with addictions to drugs or alcohol or who are being abused in some way. They help people work through big life issues like marriage, divorce, and career change. The job often involves working with patients who have mental illnesses or behavioral disorders.

The most common way that psychologists help people is through talking (and listening!). Using different types of talk **therapy**, psychologists help patients better understand their feelings and work through their problems. Psychologists also use tests and other tools to help uncover issues and diagnose problems.

Psychologists often specialize in working with specific types of patients, such as children, military veterans, or the elderly. Sports psychologists help motivate athletes toward peak performance. Animal psychologists work with pets that have behavior or anxiety problems.

Check It Out!

Find out all you can about how brains work at

- http://bit.ly/GeniusBrain
- http://bit.ly/BrainKids
- http://bit.ly/InsidetheMind

Start Now!

- ✔ Look into becoming a peer mediator at your school.
- ✔ Talk to your school counselor about what it is like to do his or her job.
- ✔ Keep a "feelings" journal to see how your emotions affect how you behave.

SURGEON

Surgeons are medical doctors who have years of training and experience. Their job is to open up the human body to repair, remove, or replace injured or diseased parts. This work takes steady hands, nerves of steel, and vast knowledge of how the human body works.

Surgeries involve lots of blood and guts. Those with a tendency to pass out at the sight of blood may want to think twice about becoming a surgeon. Thanks to new technologies, however, many surgeries these days don't require cutting open the body. Those with a desire to use top-notch medical skills and amazing high-tech equipment to save lives should keep reading.

There are many different kinds of surgeons. General surgeons do work that ranges from removing a child's tonsils to emergency surgeries on accident victims. Some surgeons specialize in specific areas. Cardiac surgeons operate on hearts. Brain surgeons, also called neurosurgeons, operate on brains. Some surgeons specialize in surgeries involving children. This is called pediatric surgery. Others remove cancerous tumors from the body. This specialty is called oncology.

Surgeons perform some of the most dangerous and difficult procedures in medicine. People put their lives in the hands of surgeons every day.

Check It Out!

Explore the wonders of the human body at

▶ http://bit.ly/KidsHealthBody

▶ http://bit.ly/NatGeoBody

Start Now!

✔ Say hello to the human body! Make a huge poster of the body and label all the major systems and organs.

✔ Interview your parents and friends about any surgeries they have experienced.

✔ Ask the school media specialist to help you find a kid-friendly anatomy atlas. Use it to find out more about how the human body works.

VETERINARIAN

There's a reason why "**veterinarian**" ranks high on the career wish lists of so many people. The job involves getting paid to take care of animals! Whether it's family pets, farm livestock, or zoo animals, veterinarians spend their days in the company of furry or feathered friends.

Just like doctors who treat humans, veterinarians diagnose and treat diseases, repair injuries, and perform surgery. They also work hard to prevent diseases with wellness check-ups and vaccinations. Time spent educating their patients' caregivers about how to take good care of their pets is always considered time well spent.

The biggest difference in treating humans and animals is communication. Since animals can't talk, veterinarians approach patient care as if they were detectives trying to solve a mystery. They look for clues, run tests, and put all the pieces together to make a final diagnosis.

Veterinarians need lots of training to qualify for their jobs. They start by getting a college degree. Then they must complete another four years of vet school. Lots of people want to be veterinarians, so it can be tough to get accepted into a vet school. It helps to have experience working with animals at a farm, pet store, or animal shelter or by volunteering at a zoo.

Check It Out!

Visit some of your favorite zoos online at

➡ https://nationalzoo.si.edu

➡ http://zoo.sandiegozoo.org

➡ https://www.stlzoo.org

Start Now!

✔ Start a dog-walking business in your neighborhood.

✔ Take on the responsibility of caring for your family's pet.

✔ Find out all you can about the different breeds of dogs and cats.

Acupuncturist • Allergist • Administrative services manager • Ambulance driver • Anthologist • **ATHLETIC TRAINER** • Audiologist • Billing clerk • Bioinfomatics specialist • Biostatistician • Biologist • Biomedical engineer • Cardiologist • Certified nurse assistant • Chiropractor • Claims adjuster • Clinical data manager • Clinical lab technician • Clinical pharmacologist • Clinical psychologist • Clinical research coordinator • Community health worker • Coroner • Critical care nurse • Cytotechnologist • Dental lab technician • Dentist • Dermatologist • Diagnostic medical sonographer • Dietician

WoW Big List

Take a look at some of the different kinds of jobs people do in the Health Sciences pathway.   **WoW!**

Some of these job titles will be familiar to you. Others will be so unfamiliar that you will scratch your head and say "huh?"

• **EMERGENCY MEDICAL TECHNICIAN** • ENT specialist • Environmental health scientist • Epidemiologist • Family practitioner • Geneticist • Gynecologist • Health educator • Health service manager • Histotechnologist • Home health aide • Hospitalist • Immunologist • Internist • Language therapist • Licensed practical nurse • Massage therapist • Medical assistant • Medical service manager • Medical doctor • Medical equipment representative • Medical laboratory technician • Medical records technician • Medical transcriptionist • Midwife • MRI technologist • Naturopathic physician • Neurodiagnostic technologist • Neurologist • Nuclear medicine technician • Nurse practitioner • **NUTRITIONIST** • Obstetrician • Occupational therapist • Oncologist • Optician • Optometrist • Oral surgeon • **ORTHODONTIST** • Orthotist • Orderly • Paramedic • Pathologist • Pediatrician • Pharmacist • Pharmacy technician • Physical therapist • **PHYSICIAN'S ASSISTANT**

Find a job title that makes you curious. Type the name of the job into your favorite Internet search engine and find out more about the people who have that job.

1 What do they do?

2 Where do they work?

3 How much training do they need to do this job?

• Plastic surgeon • Podiatrist • Prosthetist • **PSYCHOLOGIST** • Psychiatrist • Public health administrator • Radiologist • Registered nurse • Regulatory affairs director • Respiratory therapy technician • Research scientist • Rheumatologist • Sonographer • Speech pathologist • Sports medicine physician • Substance abuse social worker • **SURGEON** • Urologist • **VETERINARIAN** • X-ray technician

TAKE YOUR PICK

	Put stars next to your 3 favorite career ideas	Put an X next to the career idea you like the least	Put a question mark next to the career idea you want to learn more about
Athletic Trainer			
Emergency Medical Technician			
Nutritionist			
Orthodontist			
Physician's Assistant			
Psychologist			
Surgeon			
Veterinarian			
	What do you like most about these careers?	What is it about this career that doesn't appeal to you?	What do you want to learn about this career? Where can you find answers?
	Which Big Wow List ideas are you curious about?		

Please do **NOT** write in this book if it doesn't belong to you. You can download a copy of this activity online at www.cherrylakepublishing.com/activities.

EXPLORE SOME MORE

The Health Sciences pathway is only one of 16 career pathways that hold exciting options for your future. Take a look at the other 15 to figure out where to start exploring next.

 ## Architecture and Construction

WOULD YOU ENJOY making things with LEGOs™, building a treehouse or birdhouse, or designing the world's best skate park?

CAN YOU IMAGINE someday working at a construction site, a design firm, or a building company?

ARE YOU CURIOUS ABOUT what civil engineers, demolition technicians, heavy-equipment operators, landscape architects, or urban planners do?

 ## Arts & Communications

WOULD YOU ENJOY drawing your own cartoons, using your smartphone to make a movie, or writing articles for the student newspaper?

CAN YOU IMAGINE someday working at a Hollywood movie studio, a publishing company, or a television news station?

ARE YOU CURIOUS ABOUT what actors, bloggers, graphic designers, museum curators, or writers do?

 ## Business & Administration

WOULD YOU ENJOY playing Monopoly, being the boss of your favorite club or team, or starting your own business?

CAN YOU IMAGINE someday working at a big corporate headquarters, government agency, or international business center?

ARE YOU CURIOUS ABOUT what brand managers, chief executive officers, e-commerce analysts, entrepreneurs, or purchasing agents do?

 ## Education & Training

WOULD YOU ENJOY babysitting, teaching your grandparents how to use a computer, or running a summer camp for neighbor kids in your backyard?

CAN YOU IMAGINE someday working at a college counseling center, corporate training center, or school?

ARE YOU CURIOUS ABOUT what animal trainers, coaches, college professors, guidance counselors, or principals do?

 Finance

WOULD YOU ENJOY earning and saving money, being the class treasurer, or playing the stock market game?

CAN YOU IMAGINE someday working at an accounting firm, bank, or Wall Street stock exchange?

ARE YOU CURIOUS ABOUT what accountants, bankers, fraud investigators, property managers, or stockbrokers do?

Food & Natural Resources

WOULD YOU ENJOY exploring nature, growing your own garden, or setting up a recycling center at your school?

CAN YOU IMAGINE someday working at a national park, raising crops in a city farm, or studying food in a laboratory?

ARE YOU CURIOUS ABOUT what landscape architects, chefs, food scientists, environmental engineers, or forest rangers do?

Government

WOULD YOU ENJOY reading about U.S. presidents, running for student council, or helping a favorite candidate win an election?

CAN YOU IMAGINE someday working at a chamber of commerce, government agency, or law firm?

ARE YOU CURIOUS about what mayors, customs agents, federal special agents, intelligence analysts, or politicians do?

Hospitality & Tourism

WOULD YOU ENJOY traveling, sightseeing, or meeting people from other countries?

CAN YOU IMAGINE someday working at a convention center, resort, or travel agency?

ARE YOU CURIOUS ABOUT what convention planners, golf pros, tour guides, resort managers, or wedding planners do?

Human Services

WOULD YOU ENJOY showing a new kid around your school, organizing a neighborhood food drive, or being a peer mediator?

CAN YOU IMAGINE someday working at an elder care center, fitness center, or mental health center?

ARE YOU CURIOUS ABOUT what elder care center directors, hairstylists, personal trainers, psychologists, or religious leaders do?

Information Technology

WOULD YOU ENJOY creating your own video game, setting up a Web site, or building your own computer?

CAN YOU IMAGINE someday working at an information technology start-up company, software design firm, or research and development laboratory?

ARE YOU CURIOUS ABOUT what artificial intelligence scientists, big data analysts, computer forensic investigators, software engineers, or video game designers do?

⚖️ Law & Public Safety

WOULD YOU ENJOY working on the school safety patrol, participating in a mock court trial at school, or coming up with a fire escape plan for your home?

CAN YOU IMAGINE someday working at a cyber security company, fire station, police department, or prison?

ARE YOU CURIOUS ABOUT what animal control officers, coroners, detectives, firefighters, or park rangers do?

⚙️ Manufacturing

WOULD YOU ENJOY figuring out how things are made, competing in a robot-building contest, or putting model airplanes together?

CAN YOU IMAGINE someday working at a high-tech manufacturing plant, engineering firm, or global logistics company?

ARE YOU CURIOUS ABOUT what chemical engineers, industrial designers, supply chain managers, robotics technologists, or welders do?

Marketing

WOULD YOU ENJOY keeping up with the latest fashion trends, picking favorite TV commercials during Super Bowl games, or making posters for a favorite school club?

CAN YOU IMAGINE someday working at an advertising agency, corporate marketing department, or retail store?

ARE YOU CURIOUS ABOUT what creative directors, market researchers, media buyers, retail store managers, and social media consultants do?

 Science, Technology, Engineering & Mathematics (STEM)

WOULD YOU ENJOY concocting experiments in a science lab, trying out the latest smartphone, or taking advanced math classes?

CAN YOU IMAGINE someday working in a science laboratory, engineering firm, or research and development center?

ARE YOU CURIOUS ABOUT what aeronautical engineers, ecologists, statisticians, oceanographers, or zoologists do?

✈️ Transportation

WOULD YOU ENJOY taking pilot or sailing lessons, watching a NASA rocket launch, or helping out in the school carpool lane?

CAN YOU IMAGINE someday working at an airport, mass transit system, or shipping port?

ARE YOU CURIOUS ABOUT what air traffic controllers, flight attendants, logistics planners, surveyors, and traffic engineers do?

MY WoW

I am here.

_____
Name

_____
Grade

_____
School

Who I am.

Make a word collage! Use 5 adjectives to form a picture that describes who you are.

Where I'm going.

The next career pathway I want to explore is

_____

Some things I need to learn first to succeed.

1 _____

2 _____

3 _____

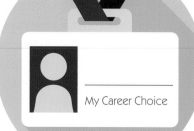

_____
My Career Choice

To get here.

GLOSSARY

athletic trainer
person who is a certified health care professional who practices in the field of sports medicine

bicuspids
teeth with two points, located beside the front sets of upper and lower teeth

cancer
serious disease in which some cells in the body grow faster than normal cells and destroy healthy organs and tissues

canines
the pointed teeth located on the side of the upper and lower jaws

diabetes
disease in which there is too much sugar in the blood

diagnose
to determine what disease a patient has or what the cause of a problem is

emergency medical technician
person who is specially trained and certified to administer basic emergency services to victims of trauma or acute illness before and during transportation to a hospital or other health care facility

fellowship
medical training that teaches doctors a sub-specialty, such as internal medicine or pediatric hematology

health sciences
all the jobs involved in planning, managing, and providing health care

incisors
teeth located in the front of the mouth that are used for cutting

molars
wide, flat teeth at the back of the mouth used for crushing and chewing food

nutritionist
person whose job is to give advice on how food affects your health

obesity
the condition of being extremely overweight

orthodontist
a type of dentist who specializes in straightening crooked teeth

paramedic
person trained to give emergency medical treatment

physician's assistant
person certified to provide basic medical services usually under the supervision of a licensed physician

psychologist
person who is trained to study and evaluate behavior and mental processes

surgeon
physician who treats disease or injury by performing surgeries

veterinarian
person who treats diseases, disorders, and injuries in nonhuman animals

INDEX

* Refers to the Web page sources

About the Author

Diane Lindsey Reeves is the author of lots of children's books. She has written several original PEANUTS stories (published by Regnery Kids and Sourcebooks). She is especially curious about what people do and likes to write books that get kids thinking about all the cool things they can be when they grow up. She lives in Cary, North Carolina, and her favorite thing to do is play with her grandkids—Conrad, Evan, Reid, and Hollis Grace.